The City Belongs To Me

People said to me
    why did you run for mayor?
And I said
    because it is my city.
People said to me
    but you aren't a politician
    or a lawyer.
And I said I am a poet.
    The city belongs to me.

HARNETT
Democrat for Mayor

Campaign poster, 197

Dedication

To Lila --

who lead the parade;

To Claire --

who scrounged the signatures;

To Marge --

who spoke the right tongues

To all those who helped

and voted for me

I tip my heart.

Why

did I run for Mayor
people ask. The answer
is in these poems
though I'm not sure
which one. Unpoetically,
with the help of Gordon Marshall,
I sued the SEC, under the
Freedom of Information Act, to
force out the truth of how the
city's finances were botched.
I campaigned while Son of Sam
marauded, blackouts
darkened the streets
unleashing savagery
and terrorists left their calling
cards. This was 1977. The
campaign was ultimately won by Koch.
It was the beginning of what turned out
to be the golden age of political corruption
in New York City.

1

The Return

Coming In

At night the Jersey coast
was a glowing lifeline
on the palm of the sea.
The land filled in
with flashing veins
and crimson creases
as the plane edged toward the
city of the dream --
        the gypsy dream
where fame and fortune and despair
shone in rising splendor
under the wings.

Crossing The
Queensboro Bridge

Early morning, through a trellis of steel,
  blinking back at me
bloodshot eyes awake the city.
Clouds plume the chimneys.
Brushes of light rim the grey.
  Here and there
a building, a sign, a water tower
presents itself for blessing.
  Down the river
Manhattan rises from a pocket of mist
marbles in the hand of earth
  ready for play.

The Return

Ellis Island is a montage
face
after
face
after
face
after
face
this thread
that binds our dead.
Sunset
bloodies the waters
the color of liberty.
Memories coil
on rotted benches
filthy latrines.
Symbols hunch on the rusting hinges
of hapless doors -
once the gates of golden triumph.
Wind
rattling the corridors
provokes no real concern
for the memories
for the symbols
for the faces who were there
and will someday return.
All is ready
steady in the hand of our history
for the return.

A Bridge

This bridge of sighs
this bridge of lies
weaves a portent
in my eyes.

This phantom bridge
threading mist
imprints your seal
with pulsing steel.

I've seen it before
a thousand times
      (and will again)
this treachery
this memory.

Shadows drown
in the river's fold.
I hear their cries
and just grow old.

The New York Times/Neal Boenzi

Mario M. Cuomo and Mayor Beame exchanging remarks during debate. The candidates, from left: Representative Herman Badillo, Joel Harnett, Mr. Cuomo, Representative Edward I. Koch, Percy E. Sutton, Mr. Beame, Bella S. Abzug.

BANKERS DENOUNCE SOME LANCE MOVES

Overdrafts Among Acts Held Not Typical or Ethically Acceptable

By MICHAEL C. JENSEN

A number of Bert Lance's banking practices fell outside the limits of customary or even ethically acceptable behavior, according to bankers and financial executives who were asked in a spot check to assess the embattled budget director's performance as a Georgia banker.

The bankers' views are considered pertinent because one of Mr. Lance's basic defenses against allegations of impropriety has been that he conducted his affairs in typical banker-like fashion. In addition, President Carter has specifically defended his budget director's banking activities.

Some of the bankers who were interviewed defended as relatively commonplace a few of Mr. Lance's practices that have come under attack, such as his borrowing from correspondent banks at relatively low interest rates.

Most of them sharply denounced other actions, however, particularly the massive bank overdrafts by Mr. Lance and his relatives—some of them used to help finance his unsuccessful campaign for Governor of Georgia. The overdrafts, at one time totaling $450,000, were described by one banker as "unconscionable" because of their size.

The bankers, in the course of discussing Mr. Lance's financial activities, disclosed much about the banking industry

Continued on Page D3, Col. 1

Democratic Mayoral Rivals Hold Debate Filled With Recriminations

By FRANK LYNN

Pointing up the personality issue in the mayoral primary campaign, Democratic candidates attacked one another's integrity, honesty and qualifications yesterday in a debate that often slipped into finger-jabbing shouting matches.

In a three-hour session at The New York Times a week before the primary, the candidates, normally not given to public displays of emotion, clashed angrily and often on such issues as capital punishment, the fiscal crisis, the blackout and looting, education, help for the city's poor and Governor Carey's support of Mario M. Cuomo in the primary.

Of the seven candidates, only Representative Herman Badillo refrained from personal attacks on his opponents.

Times Misquoted Carey

An article and a headline in The Times yesterday incorrectly quoted Governor Carey as saying Mayor Beame lacked the "integrity" to run the city during the 1974-75 fiscal crisis. Mr. Carey's actual words were: "I did my utmost to find in the incumbent the kind of leadership our city needed. For whatever reason, it wasn't there."

The Governor's intervention, touched off one of the most explosive—but not untypical—exchanges when Mr. Cuomo, his face contorted by anger, and feverishly wagging his finger, shouted: "Bella, you're lying, you're lying, you're lying and you're good at it."

The New York Secretary of State was demanding that Mrs. Abzug prove her

Excerpts from the debate, page B4.

contention that Governor Carey had telephoned newspapers to disclose Mr. Cuomo's candidacy.

Several of the candidates agreed that the session was the most vituperative of their meetings so far. Without television cameras to keep them on their good behavior, they let their hair down as their tempers flared, as one of the candidates noted.

The clashes revealed more than the candidates' tempers. Representative Edward I. Koch was the most frequent target of the angry words, an indication that his opponents feel he has moved into strong contention from a position far back in the field two months ago.

Three other candidates, Mayor Beame,

Continued on Page B5, Col. 1

China Reversing Education Policy To Improve the Quality of Schools

By FOX BUTTERFIELD
Special to The New York Times

HONG KONG, Sept. 1—Peking's new smiles about it," Professor Lieberthal

2

Our Times

Our Times

Rising
each a.m.
to the front door
to pick up our Times
a quotidian round
of good news, bad news
      same news;
so to suck, so to grunt
so to pass away
a yesterday
and start again another day.

Out of the night
that covers me
black as a pit
from pole to pole
I thank whatever Gods
may be
for the morning Times
that liberates me
from my insomniac
soul.

I am a hunter
foraging.
I have not seen a **dinosaur**
or **buffalo** tracks;
yet I sense leads.
I keep my eyes sharp.

I sneeze 12 times
each time
I read The Sunday Times--
an allergy to ink
        paper
or the editorials?

Robert Birmelin

"On 14th St. after the Jewelry Store Robbery"

Courtesy Sherry French Gallery, NY

3

On The Street

On The Street

Down the country western block.
Up the big band street.
Into the jazz
The zither promenade-
6th Avenue, Avenue of the Americas.
This sunny, teeming musical mall
where pale musicians pit their hunger
against your generosity
their art against your will
my minutes between appointments
their concert hall.

Out the door, seconds after she fe
now sheet-covered.
The paramedic ambulance arrive:
in a siren of futility.
Now Diaz mops up the moisture
where the body lay.

blazing bandana wrapped around
r beehive crown.
ashing anger in a sea of blue makeup
op a swirl of silk scarves
lling, this black lady,
r the Ku Klux Klan
   clean up New York.

Racing toward me, down 41st,
the mob screaming, stop him.
Dodges one man, Then another.
A desperate kid. Right at me.
Will I...
Ten feet away.
A figure lurches toward him,
   in tennis shoes
but wears a badge.
Falls in a heap five feet away.
Would I have stopped him?
Would you?

Bertha's Day

Be cheerful said the minister
and the body before him was serene.
Will someone come **forward**
with a congregational hymn of happiness?
- No sadness now
said the minister
and the body before him was serene.
No one came foward.
Then the chorus sang Hold The Line
- Hold the line for Jesus.
They were his people here.
Not an empty seat.
Not a single soul incorrectly dressed.
A stunning solemnity.
Nor did the minister say a word
of how it happened or why.
He talked of Job and the pain
he endured; of mystery, the impossibility
of knowing the unknown
or asking why.
She, a nurse, had purchased tickets
at the Brooklyn Academy of Music
for herself and Bertha
her mother, a celebration.

The slasher attacked repeatedly
in her home, only an hour later
the body discovered by her child,
four years of age. Now so old.
In a single line, a processional,
I walked towards the body
and saw it was serene and young
the child herself of a mother
who I saw fleetingly behind her veil;
a face I knew as smiling
now dark and wrinkled,
indistinct. Was she Bertha?
Then a tremor, a recognition
and for a moment we knew each other
as we were and never again will be.

Later in the street I saw houses
coming down, going up,
the repairing of a soul.
The slasher walks these streets.
So does his assassin.

Hallucination

At 5 AM
      on the city street
the grey, relentless scuttle
      of a garbage truck;
teams of beings filing
      house to house
scavenging for bodies
      after the night's carnage;
back and forth
      sacks across their backs
assiduous
      in the early morning haze
the grinding wheeze of the pulverizer
      their sound track.

On The Street

Ah! Toro
the matador
with contemptuous stare
bewilders the beast
Then cooly withdraws -
      and the raging taxi
      lurches to a halt
      before the lady's
      disdainful eye.

Marty!
I thought your were dead-
so alive you are
recycled, subway token in hand.
Chips of life, endlessly flaking.

My city myself
people traffic politics
intersecting in me
and the red light
green light rush
of my time.

Weather Watch

Not quite hidden
in her translucent umbrella gloom
was she pondering
life, duty, love?
        sailing the rain-washed streets
        a bark of unquestioned beauty.

Back-slapped by icy winds
straining the fabric of my shearling
I saw the woolen, fashioned skirt
deeply slit to curving thighs
gulping in frigid blasts
and imagined a rouged and refrigerated
        behind.

The corner was a bowling alley for the wind
whistling and whooping.
Hassled people sucked in air
insulating themselves.
I smiled in brotherly fortitude
a man smiled back
She
        with the foxy coat, pepper blond hair
        and reddened face
iced the wind with rejection.

City Sky

I encounter you
city sky
red   pale   pink
draping streeted aisles
where balcony teeth
snip your flowering folds.
Glass towers cube
your frosty air
yet, soaring, barely touch your
red   pale   pink.
They are prisms
scattering rainbow rays
of glowing dust
icy color, serenely polluted
red   pale   pink.
You bend the skyscrapers
cap the rivers
parade the honking avenues
where people
       dodging fate
suck in your glory
      and wait.

The Region / Continued

The Democratic mayoralty candidates brave the summer heat: from left, top row, Mario M. Cuomo, Percy E. Sutton, and Edward I. Koch; front row, Mayor Beame (with a young constituent), Herman Badillo (with an anonymous supporter), Bella S. Abzug (with an impromptu dance partner) and Joel W. Harnett.

Photos by Richard Kalvar/Magnum for The New York Times

Summertime and the Campaigning Isn't Easy

By MAURICE CARROLL

Leaning on a bulky bundle of nominating petitions, Percy E. Sutton grinned at the reporters who were standing behind the counter at the Board of Elections office to watch that ritual event of New York politics—The Presentation of the Petitions.

"Actually, I came by to see my friends," Mr. Sutton said silkily. "I see so little of you out there in the streets when I'm campaigning. And I suspected that you might be here. So I came by to say hello."

He grinned again. But with the politeness that is his oratorical style, Mr. Sutton was underlining a fact of life for summertime politicians. In their pursuit of attention (which they seek on the theory that it will help remind voters that they are around), candidates often must reverse the presumed procedure in which reporters seek news. Instead, they seek reporters.

Only politicians care much about politics when the summer sun shines, but this year primary day follows Labor Day by only three days and the people who aspire to New York City office must be inventive attention-getters.

So they nibble hot dogs at Nathan's and knishes on the Lower East Side and cannoli in Little Italy. They squeeze through beach-club crowds greasy with sun-tan lotion and confront small children who menacingly brandish cotton candy or leaking ice cream cones.

Every year at about this stage of the pre-campaign, politicians and reporters begin telling each other that there never has been an election to match this one in dullness, that everyone is on vacation, that no one cares. Even discounting that, the 1977 election does seem, so far, at least to be more of a ho-hum than in recent memory. Remember the Mario Biaggi's candidacy that was blown away by revelations about grand jury testimony, when John V. Lindsay lost Republican primary and pieced together scheduled endorsement by the Democrats on his way to victory as a Liberal? Or the hot primary say came on the Democratic side of the city? Or 1965, when Robert F. Wagner ran again?

This time, most people who rate the field of seven announced mayoral candidates rank them high on quality but, with the possible exception of Bella Abzug, low on charisma. Still, they try.

Edward I. Koch has a "Koch-mobile," his press people said. Herman Badillo holds a news conference, and other candidates arrive. Mario Cuomo joins the orches-

tra. Percy Sutton tours with Muhammad Ali. Joel Harnett trails around town wearing a "Harnett For Mayor" T-shirt.

Oddly, and only in part because the incumbent can command the attention of the cameramen, Mayor Beame seems to be matching Mrs. Abzug as a political stunt pilot. Mrs. Abzug, for whom the adjective "flamboyant" might have been invented, began her campaign by—literally—throwing toward the cameras one of the big-brimmed hats that are her identification mark, then producing another hat from under the lectern. We have since enjoyed the "Bella Boogie" and a series of events designed to lure the photographers.

But it was Mr. Beame, the determinedly unspectacular bookkeeper,

the candidate? "I have no problem," Mr. Koch says. "It's out in a subway station every morning [he and Mrs. Abzug are the most diligent in that sort of work] and then off to the streets and the stores."

One must be resourceful. When rain washed out street campaigning for him last week, he directed his "Koch-mobile" to the shielded corridors of the World Trade Center, in search of vacationers. New York City candidates swing out to Long Island beaches and mountain resorts: Mrs. Abzug was in the Catskills this weekend, for instance.

Mr. Badillo insists the press has a middle-class myopia about the city, believing that everyone is at the beach for the summer. People in slums can't afford summer vacations, he says, and

4

City Life

Gallery Going

In Jack Beal's picture,
many presences --
the rubbery wrinkle
of stunning, spikey white flowers;
the worked-over work gloves
 gnarled like an old oak;
the ancient master tapestry
alive with today's youth;
himself a presence
giving life to things
and things to life.

Sidney Gooman cries Fire!
Hell on black pastel.
                    Accident!
Trucks in collision.
The terror is there.
But he cloaks it with a harmony
that turns our eyes from fear.

Bill King gawks and shrugs,
palms off life on stilted legs
and makes of them a calligraphy
of awkward grace. Which,
in its way, can be said of
Botero's pachydermic ladies.
They are stars
who glory in their daintiness,
their celebrity.
This art is in the touch,
never the shape.
Yet, together, they are a comedy act.

The leaves are turning crisp and golden
wine reds, russets, yellow green.
The bower, sheltered,
ponds and streams glowing,
bring the peace of Jasper Cropsey
the nostalgia of a cycle
ever-returning, a painting
ever new.

We think one hundred years,
a century, a long time ago.
Yet, in Bricher's
sea and shore and hazy light
on the green mountainside --
there is today, tomorrow
and all the dreams of yesterday's
content.

The Fashion Ball

Fluttering chiffon
creamy leather
slouching peacock clothes
on models who
with a calculated jauntiness
stroke the midway.
Fleeting glimpses
of name designers
the new princely caste
then interminable speeches
about the guest of honor
the man who
who responds in kind
gratefully to dissipate
in the geriatric madness
and music of my day.
So with hugs and kisses
ends the fashion ball.

Small Change

"How are you feeling today, Mr. Harnett?"
        a doorman's casual remark.
Silly question I would have thought
        when I was younger.
        Pro forma.
        Why bother to ask?
Stomach gassy, buzzing with arthritis
        (code name for aging bones)
I ponder a reply.
In his courteous way, he is asking
        about the state of my wealth,
        the coins of advancing years
        once small change.

I am grateful
        noting his steely hair
creased chin   sloping shoulder.
"And how are you feeling?"
and light up my moment
        with his smile.

At The Coffee Shop

Change comes
in crumpled bills

edges squashed
and rippled

each one
patiently fingered,

no slick
bankers bucks

deftly flicked
from a fresh deck.

Morning Museum

The Chock Full of Nuts
is a mighty museum
of morning art
full of Tookers
glazed-eye sleepers
chomping
      plain doughnuts
         slurping coffee
in a dazed infinity

One girl sparkles
primps her hair
looks around expectantly
         She lives.

At Sotheby's

Seized by the disease
of the auction show,
ranting, raving
until the hammer's blow
I bust the bounds
of legacy
in a truly aesthetic
bankruptcy.

Next time you go
to an auction show
strap your arms
to either hip
bite your lip
don't even quiver
or you'll find yourself
a winning bidder.

5

Hanging On

Jerome Witkin
"On the R&R"
Courtesy of NYNEX, White Plains, N.Y.

Subway's
tendril
threat
silent
wordless
vining
grimy windows
walls
vicious in
profusion
                    Rattle on
Tracks
of steel
etched
on foreheads —
lips
charming
jolting demons
with violent
empty
phrases
                    Rattle on
Cramped
mosaic
people
papers up
books down
their fortress
skulls
besieged
by screeching
forces
                    Hanging on

Subway

I stride among the girders
hearing the rolling subway thunder.
People of all nations are arrayed against me,
their mark on the floors or sides of cars.
They have their art; shattered tiles forming mosaics,
stands of disappearing steel,
pitted, dirty, neon-lit by Marlboro men
marching to a tawdry infinity.

Listen, said the man to a woman.
"On the street I sell these watches
for $55. Here I sell them for $35."
Lower overhead, I pondered.
"The cops do not bother me
here," he said.

No "B" train.
A loudspeaker, drowning in discord,
explained unheard alternatives.

On this train
vines of graffitti
slithered, slashed and clawed
every map, every window,
every door, every ceiling
of every car, suffocating hope.
Life turned against itself;
Life a charnal house;
Life without control except an insatiable greed for life.
Now and then I saw a face
Memories, flashing, reborn.

Once, I saw men punched out
knifed through. I dreamed
with her riding back to Brooklyn.
I saw the Irish threaten the Jews,
the tired slope in release. A cast of old,.
young, fat, negro
white, Italian, Greek. I heard
the rickety, rackety echo of
the place and saw the patient,
vacant, facade of faces
wanting, waiting for their freedom.

Then I saw a man who died
I know he died but there he walked
through turnstiles and down the steps
along the platform, paper in hand.
Alive again, flaked off the thick ooze
        of life, a resurrection.

This is an efficient ride, cheap at the price.
It takes me where I want to go.
It works and this is a miracle.

Day after day it burrows its way
among the rocks and slime of underground
suddenly rearing into triumphant light.

Day after day it sucks in the fearful masses
doors mashing pulverizing egos.

continued

When the sun has set and light plays on reddened waters
when it is quiet on earth and beauty
steps out like a graceful woman from her bath
when the water laps the shore
and the coming night releases its first chill breath
It rattles and jolts. It stalls and delays.
It wheezes in agonies of metal and goes on.

I knew a secret.
There was a gum machine on Dekalb Avenue
that coughed out its product free.
And, if I were in the right car, in the right place
I could race out as the door opened,
cash it in, then race back before it closed
continuing on to my accordion lesson.

It took me to Ebbets Field. To Sheepshead Bay.
To 42nd Street and plates of spaghetti at Romeo's.
I was too embarrassed, as a kid, to duck under
                                    the turnstiles.
The bad ones did. Or were they the brave?

Still it rattles. Still it heaves
Always singing its sad steel song
of slouching, sagging people, pressing on
                                    hanging on
sleeping out the stations, the raucous cycle
of a dwindling life.

6

Making It

On Grand Central

Mercury winced
at joggers who a year ago
could hardly bend a knee
What is Mercury
if not speed - whined the woman
and you are stoned.

Nor did Mercury object
when Pan American
pinched her backside.
(Women, he rationalized,
are more easily discomforted than men.)
Did not Pan American
enhance his glory?

Now Mercury squints,
buildings to the left
buildings to the right
shades of diminishing light
tunneling his domain.
What indignities to come
intones the lady.

Mercury shrugs: Who cares?
He is the messenger of the Gods.
Until they call he must wait
knowing too well even they
could no more silence a woman
than stop construction in New York.

Empire State

Shape of failure
or hope--
what's your point?

Avant garde
or retard--
what's your point?

Marker for the road ahead
or already tread--
what's your point?

At The Empire Base

Skyward
nightward
through its bonnet
tissue white
trembling with light
the ebony blade
soars
in sudden
suspense-
guardian
of the city
night.

    Hot pants
    hookers
    silver bottomed
    hookers
    levied
    hookers
    corralled
    by a white hat
    pimp
    citizens all
    and so are you
    and I
    and all of us
    at the Empire base
    cadging
    parking spots

near darkened
churches
synagogues
mosques
seeking the greek
    where
emerald-skirted
flashing silks
and sequins
cymbals snapping
black hair swirling
whirling
to the bouzouki's
driving
pattern sound
spider's lacework
framing
her bare belly
shimmering belly
(My God
an appendectomy
would scar
her out of business)
the belly dancer
is showered
with dollar bills
    and
turlu
anghinar

shish kebob
shishlak
baklava
passa dava
moussakka
leap from the menus
in neigborhoods
where slit-skirted
dusky thighs
patrol their beats
more faithfully
than cops
and the bouzouki
drives
        ripples
                swells --
spills
croons
        to the Balkan
        and the Greek
        and the Israeli
        and the Turk
        and the Yemenite
        and the Arab
        and the beat
                is heard
        on the floor
        on the street

in the business deal
and the massage
                parlor
wherever the dagger
                falls
and later on
arm in arm
when the men dance
I see
that time of years
ago, that time
                of night
when the hours sighed
and I searched the cruise
ship for a drink
and found instead
locked arm in arm
        swaying
                singing
        matching steps
                gliding
in greek cadence
the cabin boys
while the ship sailed
into the silver water
of the golden
                Mediterranean
                        dawn.

Afterwards

Over the banks of Seagram Plaza
I watch the waves slipping over
        Park Ave. shore
while the thump of the bass fiddle
        and soft piano
while the echo of bouzouki and its
        Bosphorous score
flare through the fountains, flare
        through the dawn.
A paper bag strums the stuttering
        wind.
Dim lights play chess on hunching
        tower squares.
People stretch and lay their languid
        mood
over the banks, over the shore, over
        the cages
that lie beneath and in the air
        and in the towers
soon to explode, savage beasts to prey
        on a feeding city.

But Above All Things
Truth
Beareth Away the Victor*

The pigeon sits
on the lion's nose.
The lion in its
infinite tolerance
manages a smile.
So the pigeon
twits the lion's nose.
The lion knows
it is king
and the king
must maintain
dignity at all times -
especially with the likes of a pigeon.

* Inscription on stone on
  the NY Public Library

Palm Court

I hear violins
and the murmur of good people
pondering their polished plates
and rich desserts.
The lights are silken
the arched and figured ceilings high-
The hour late.
Demure young waitresses
loiter in old world luxury.

I have found a peace,
surrogate for romance
with muted sounds and things and surfaces
and the ebb of energy.
This night.
      This place.
           This passionless ease.

Freedom

Playing tennis into the night
under Town Tennis Club lights;
shredded grey clouds
scud the towering white whale
and the dim summer breeze
breathes up balm.
                                 Recall
the public parks, basketball into dust
        straining to see the hoop
baseball into twilight shadow -
        come home! come home!

And now no one to lock the gate
        turn out the lights
        or call it a night.
And now, in the same city, in the same night
        a dream apart.
        freedom lives.

History

I will tell you anything for a vote
for winning grants me historical note.
Despite the lying, it's quite satisfying
to count yourself undying.

Long after you've forgotten what I said
or didn't; indeed after you're dead
some scholar will discover my name
and, pen in hand, declare its fame.

With reputation aching to be made
he'll stroke the fires of my grade;
how, secretly, I did do much
(and read the book to keep in touch).

Historians, like politicians, pay their dues:
who gets the vote, makes the news.
Immortality isn't for the proud -
Only those who work the crowd.

7

People

Princess

She was a Jewess
brown-eyed and voluptuous.
There was promise
of tribal intercourse
of UJA and temple boards
of ritual sex
all warmth and spun with psalms
and undertones of guilt.
She, an achiever, wished
    a mink coat
    a decorated apartment
    to travel.
She sang. She sought contacts.
She had energy.
And she made decisions
one of which was to be friends.

Now and then I will think of her
as a pleasant afternoon
spent with royalty.

The Lawyer

The real, the mighty
The bushy-tailed
armed combatant of our day
brief-case charged
statute-equipped
modern Maginot
and mobile striking force.
In politics he clicks.
None better.
He legislates and regulates
mostly he equivocates.
He writes our laws
without flaws, I think.
Siphon is he
of our warring energy;
grease in our wheels.
We pay homage
with unfathomed fees
in swelling seas.
Win or lose
he wins. With a grin.
A gentleman.
Salute him!

Psychiatrist

The psychiatrist
stared at me
with a clinical eye.
His son, for a decade
though highly-talented,
could not hold a job.
What was the reason?
I awaited his learned reply.
"A big mouth," he said.
Paused. Then repeated it.
Not a diagnosis I expected.
                    Clearly
the work of a psychiatrist
one respects.

Bankers

Bankers
are cautious folk
afraid of going broke

whose money
is only lent
where it won't be spent

to people
who refuse to ask
and don't **need** cash.

Copywriter

This person
with the pencil prodding his groin
is scheming equally
to avoid writing an advertisement
and to inviting fate to confer genius
at least an idea.
He is revolutionary.
He will unleash upon the unwary
greed, lust and magic bullets of envy.
Not even Karl Marx
who creates in the adjoining cubicle
can inflict such fury.
It is his images, recklessly spun-
sex, house, car, job, position, conquest-
that seep into the cracks of our restless souls...

Torment our times
make politicians heel
and armies march
in ranks of advertised desire.

Put this man in chains
or we will be joggers in the night.
An endless marathon.
Put away his pencil
and let us rest.

Behold The Scientists

On the left
stoking the genetic code
          bizarre assemblies
to change a life
or stirring juices
to make one.
          Hard workers!

On the right
tinkering with atoms
that go cosmic
          boom
enriching our experience
by thinning out
the human crop.
          Such diligence!

Left ignores right.
          Curious -
There is a facial relation.
          Cousins?
They seem unacquainted.
Are they schizo?
          Possibly.
Their special delusion
          objectivity
          operational term
          now a prayer.

How serious these ceaseless strivers!
Observed yet unobserved
immune to contagions
          of self-consciousness
job-oriented to a fault -
          what harm in that?

Manhattan Builder

This Manhattan builder
wants to make money.
A lot of money. He's a
smart dresser and goes to
parties in clubs that once
wouldn't admit his father
even if he wasn't indicted.
His second wife is beautiful
that's why he married her.
He wears her like a prize.
She is part of the bounty.
Air, light and space
are checkers on a board
to him. He moves them
cunningly. He aims to win.
He pays off politicians
in legal and illegal ways
in big gold chips -
only the big ones count.
He knows this very well.
As a poet my assets
are locked in my soul.
His are stuck in the ground,
their meters fixed.
So I understand
why he covets height.
But I need light.

The Politician

Give me your hordes
tired and teeming
yearning to be free
and I will get
you votes.

Give me the down-
trodden, mythic masses
stampeding for liberty
and I will get
you votes.

Spring from alien
dungeons the living
refuse of mankind.
Bring them to me
and I will register
and vote them
and never again
will we
lose this district.

New York Post,
August 26, 1977

TODAY
Sunny, low 80s
TONIGHT
Clear, mid 60s
TOMORROW
Sunny, 85-90
Details, page 2

TV: PAGE 68

NEW YORK POST

FRIDAY, AUGUST 26, 1977   25 CENTS   Vol. 176, No. 238   © 1977 The New York Post Corporation   R

METRO
TODAY'S RACING

DAILY PAID
CIRCULATION
2D QUARTER 1977
609,390

SEC TELLS: BEAME GUILTY OF DECEIT

'New' notes he bought were really old ones

By JARED ROPEL

The Securities and Exchange Commission today released a devastating report accusing Mayor Beame and the major banks of misrepresentation and deceit in the sale of city securities.

The long-awaited report, which climaxes one of the most massive investigations ever undertaken by the SEC, makes no charges of outright fraud.

But it presents documentary evidence indicating that the banks and city officials—including Beame—concealed from investors an increasingly desperate fear that the city was hurtling to the brink of bankruptcy.

Focusing on financial transactions between December 1974 and March 1975, the study produces data demonstrating that the banks engaged in an intense effort to sell their perilously large holdings of the weakening city securities without telling investors what the banks actually knew about the city's deteriorating fiscal condition.

OTHER CHARGES

Although the detailed findings of the report still remained secret as press time, The Post was able to learn the major conclusions.

These specifics also emerged:

● Beame misled the public in one of his efforts to demonstrate his confidence in the city's financial future. After one note sale in March 1975,

Beame appeared at a press conference holding one of the city securities which he said he had bought for himself two weeks previously. The implication was that the Mayor had purchased one of the recently offered notes as part of his faith in the city. One source, however, said the SEC investigators learned that the note had been purchased earlier and was not part of the current sale.

NO RECORD KEPT

● No minutes were kept of a critical 1975 meeting of the Comptroller's Debt Management Committee, a group of bankers and brokers who advise the city on the sale of city debt. The financial institutions reportedly that no minutes be taken because they did not want to publicize their worry that it was becoming increasingly difficult to obtain bidders for city notes.

● Chemical Bank Vice President Herbert Charbonneau testified to the SEC that Chemical made a conscious decision to "dump" its holdings of city

Continued on Page 4

JOEL HARNETT

Harnett files SEC appeal

NYP AUG 9

Democratic mayoral candidate Joel Harnett today went to the U. S. Court of Appeals to press his campaign to get the Securities and Exchange Commission to release a secret report on city finances before the primary election.

Harnett accused the SEC of abusing the judicial process—"just to stall for time."

Last week U. S. District Court Judge Vincent Broderick ordered the SEC to let him examine portions of the investigation so he could determine whether to release the documents publicly.

The SEC appealed Broderick's decision, keeping the report secret while the appeal is pending. Harnett had sued the SEC under the Freedom of Information Act to see the report. He said in a statement that he believed the report will "rip the lid off" city politics and expose deals made between bankers and high officials in the Beame Administration.

New York Post,
August 9, 1977

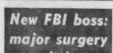

New FBI boss: major surgery
Page 7

Cause of Elvis' death hidden
Page 3

Lance called double dealer
Page 5

JOEL HARNETT   "Don't mistake me for a politician, I am a businessman

New York News World, September 6, 1

8

The City Belongs To Me

Part 1

I Was There

People said to me
      why did you run for mayor?
And I said
      because it is my city.
People said to me
      but you aren't a politician
      or a lawyer.
And I said I am a poet.
      The city belongs to me.

I will tell you something
about poetry and politics:
      The poetry doesn't get you
      any votes.
I thought indignation was
      the poetry of politics.
But now I understand
      it is arrogance.
If people believe you're too good
      for them
         you're good enough.

Image is a public truth...
      achieved
by savaging sense with nonsense
like liquidating the Lions of 42nd St.
because no one expects them to roar;
      a quotable
quickness that slides off the issue
into print.

There are verbal bullies.
Their ring is the press.
Nor can a blip society
      deal with them.

continued

Careful expression has no
                mass medium.
                Blip. Blip.
                Blip society.
Careful expression, etc...
                What about the
                errata notices
                in The New York Times?

People ask:
                "Why did you run for Mayor?"
                "I mean; why would you
                want that job?"
I answer. I am not a politician.
I am a businessman.
I want to save the city.
                They smirk:
                "You're not a politician? -
                Now you are."
And so they were right.
I could not deny it.
I am a politician now. So?
                "Then why should we believe you?"

I want to save the city.
Jesus. Moses. Buddha.
the prophet Mohammed.
 B.Young. Their aspirations
excelled mine. I prized
geographic neatness. No
need to fertilize the minds
and hearts of Hoboken. Or
Teaneck. Or New Rochelle.
Five boroughs would do.

Coming as I did
from a righteous sense of indignation
the poetry, I thought, of politics
I sought to upend the tables
of the power brokers;
Coming as I did
from years of civic study and deliberation
of speaking out on issues
anticipating deficits, even bankruptcy
(a word for poets)
I sought to bring to heel
the dogs of disaster. Start anew.
Coming as I did
the press cared little
and covered me less.
And running, I found
was fund-raising.
For in a free society
free speech is free
for those who can pay the hype.

        hype
        ripe
        for the finacial type.

But why did you run?

I an civic by nature.

I foresaw the bankruptcy of this city.
I foresaw the folly of Westway.
I foresaw the greed of municipal labor contracts.
I foresaw the absurdity of the Health and
                Hospitals Corporation.
I abjured the rise of crime and the
                decline of punishment.

continued

I wanted the children educated
I wanted to root out
               the welfare cheats
I said promote new technology
               and lower taxes
               and stop fires
               and the abandonment of buildings --
I foresaw the ineptness that created
               misery, drove out opportunity
               and laid waste human life.
I said there is a connection between politicians
               and you.
What they do and you.
And I foresaw all this as the lonely
               prophet who cried out in the desert,
               head soaking up the sun.
And I was heard
               by other candidates.

They are different than me.
They listen better.
They hear things.
I heard the bell ring true.
They heard the crack.
One day a radio broadcaster
said to me - you make
such dull speeches.

I the poet had no poetry.
No arrogance.
Had no gift to offer
except my sincerity.
But, they said, you should
have a gimmick;

      Wear all white
      Ride horseback
      Carry a mogen david
      Tear your clothes
        - beat your chest
      Curse homosexuals
Give them something
they want something.
and I give them truth
a well-known bore.

But they had capital punishment.

I proved that the citizen can
get on the ballot. Government
is of the people, not politicians
(or the lawyers who are
an occupying force).

      Question: when do you
      become a politician?

I was there.
      You could have voted for me -
      a citizen without the bosses
      or clubs
      or organizations
      nothing but a wife, a mother-in-law
      friends and tennis knees.
      I got on the ballot. You could have voted for me.

I thought I could make great sounds
and by vibrating air currents in informed ways
start stampedes and avalanches.
I thought I could deny death
and reach beyond the callosity of life.

(angels on high
fingering clouds
in heavenly orgasm)

I thought I could touch a tremor
find a flow, a pulse. Could I not
find a dream? Invent one?
Circumscribe one?

(Nothing stopped when my father
died. Not traffic. Nor doors closing.
Nor the sun in its course. Nor
pedestrians. Or tips at cafes. Or
oreo cookies. Nothing stops
until you stop.Therefore I must
go on. I must do what must be done.)

You may breathe
                    defecate
                              or worse
But you will cast no shadow on TV:
Nor will your voice be heard
from Olympus or other frequencies -
                    What are you?
                    Who are you?
                    Why are you?
If you are not known.

It was not entirely that way with me.
I had toured the TV civic ghettos
I had denounced, critiqued, acclaimed
        for hungry newscasts.
I had debated bankers and labor leaders.
I had testified before congressional committees.
When financial panic struck broadcast
        trotted me out to make sausages
        with Victor Gotbaum.
I was a whisper in the the public babble.
        Sometimes audible.

But I was not a player.

The NY Times said I would not get on the ballot.
I did. They ignored it.
The NY Post would not mention my name.
The News did. Thank you Frank Lombardi.
They thought:
        He never ran for office
        He has no political backing
        He is not rich.
        We never covered him politically before.
        We never played poker with him.

On a major TV show
newspaper reporters interviewed
me asking one question three times:
        Who will you support
        when you drop out?
Issues? Issues? Gesundheit.

So the money poured in like molasses.
Armies never enrolled.
but there were a few, enough to do.
And I did.

Part 2

Getting Organized

Got organized.
Got an office.
Got a telephone
          cash in advance.
Got a scheduler
          to tell me where to be
Got a lawyer
          to guide me on the ballot
Got field men
          to set up the posters
Got advance men
          to beat the drum
          before I come
Got TV-makers
Got policy papers
Got press secretaries
Got fund-raisers
      fund-raisers
      fund-raisers
Got on the phone
          raising funds
Got suppliers
Got a man who scratched his nose
          when I spoke too long
Get exercise
          Badillo said to me
          or your legs will go
          (I didn't. They did)
Got emissaries to
          the ethnics.
          the political clubs
Got up early
          to meet the subway crowds

continued

Got up late
        to field the night game
Get a loud-speaker
        or lose it in the larynx
Got research
        and got some truth:
        why should they vote for you?

And from the mountain
of statistics, a truth descended:
        they need a businessman
        they want a businessman
I am a businessman.
(I ask my stockholders to refrain from comment.)

They said they need jobs, lower taxes,
good management, honesty-by-God
honesty, leadership in the
fiscal wilderness, tough negotiations
with the labor unions, return to
solvency, faith in our credit, etc., etc.

Slogan:
This is not a poor city. It is poorly run.
        Can we not find happiness with a
        $12 billion dollar budget?

I am a businessman.
Logic, therefore, suggests...
But it was not a true revelation.
There was error.
Research had not read history.

Eighty years ago Lincoln Steffens
        said a politician is a business
        man with a specialty*
I did not have a specialty.
The business of politicians is to be known.
If you have not been on the score cards
you are not a player.
Nobody will bet on you.

If you have not cohabited
in the political pantheon
nobody will worship you.

If your baldness is not symbolic
it will be used this way:
        "See that guy with the skin"

Clearly I must
burst with kinetic fury
on the superscreen of public
consciousness.

Hope for a miracle.

* It is an American tradition
that successful politicians become
rich unless they start out that way.
In this process friends are made

continued

Part 3

Running

Parade

Boom! Boom! Swept the parade
past the thin ranks of summer citizens
the better part of whom, quite sensibly,
had escaped the city heat for greener parts.
Boom! Boom! It was an ethnic celebration --
bagels, pizza, souvlaki one or the other --
all the pols included, front-rank beaming
all jovial, exchanging niceties, aglow in
   civic fraternity
sopping up sun, recognition, some meager votes
when suddenly the gnomic eye of television
levelled in as the street sharply narrowed.
A hip from Herman, a lunge from Bella,
a shove from Koch, a push from Percy
even a twist from gentleman Mario --
candidates all, jostling away their dignity.
   "Is it worth it ?"
I thought slowly sucked, lashed back to a
   voteless void;
Later to hear -- Boom! Boom! -- on the 6 o'clock news
and to see those few striving, striding, elbowing
   victors
parading for all the world to see, a hard-won
haloed moment of resurrection.

continued

Astoria

There was solemnity in the candles
   of the Greek Orthodox Church
   and a sense of angels.
There was sun and candlelight
   in the eyes of the lady.
Her bosom heaved with a generosity
   of lamb and wine, nuts and raisins
   leaves stuffed with rice.
Her table of offerings shone in the darkness
   light of the square.
There were societies and stocky men
   who, courteously, wanted to know
   who had business cards, ran travel agencies.
Their eyes stroked the dancers
   who skimmed the bouzouki seas.
They were serene in their power
   in the eye of their dream.

Brighton Beach

What do they do in Brighton Beach?
They eat, they eat in Brighton Beach.
What do they do in Brighton Beach?
They talk Russian, dance to percussion.
What do they do in Brighton Beach?
They dress up babies, fatten ladies.
What do they do in Brighton Beach?
They kiss, they buzz, they drink vodka.
Ah-ha-lochka!
Whatever they're doing in Brighton Beach
I wish I was there doing it too!

Brighton Beach/Astoria

What do they do in Brighton Beach?
What do they do in Astoria?
They dream.
And when they wake
so does New York.

Bella

A pocket of mottled, sagging flesh
oozed above the silk, stressed stocking
sheathing this massive haunch, hauled
laboriously after the other on the steep steps
            to the third floor Democratic Club.
"Why do I need this?" the gasping voice.

She washed in over the seat
after the other candidates had arrived,
a tidal force, powering me off my chair.
Elbows, in rapid sequence, pounded the table
rattling dishes, spilling water.
"Why do they waste their time running
when I'm so far ahead in the polls?"
she asked the air.

Bella was Juliet on the balcony.
I was Romeo
entering a school basement for a meeting.
She cooed down to me; she sighed--
    "Be my economic commissioner."

So the crowd cheered; then she raised her fist,
another telling point; suddenly blanching --
    "I don't feel well."
Sat down, calmly finishing her remarks.
Later, blocks and intense traffic aggravation away,
I found Bella before me, strident and strong,
    driving for votes.

There was a stir in the Temple rear
as I finished my statement.
An entrance was underway, a determined
stride, the momentum of weight and pace,

the flash of a symbol (a hat),
a murmur going to a roar. "Bella is here!"
Then the applause swelling.
She was certainly here, the center aisle
    her playing field.

She honed their indignation.
The landlords.
The political hacks.
The rednecks who held back women.

The Gods in their liberal pantheon
had indeed blessed their apostle.

The faithful saluted with cheers.

Old socialism, its heros and battles
    hung spectre-like mid-air.

Then, from the floor, questions:
Welfare cheats?
Police strikes?
Punishing muggers?
Capital punishment?

She answered wrong
as she had done time after time
as she knew she had done.

As she left the podium
there was a murmur but no roar.
Ther was applause but it was polite,
cool courtesy dispatching a loser.

Old loves never die.
Nor can they endure a present passion.

Yesterday's Shadow

I sat in yesterday's shadows
      of the pavilions
            on the Coney Island boardwalk
Gloria encircled
      her pouting face
            poised, expecting
Our lips papier-mache
      dry and brittle-
            where was sensation?
Overhead fireworks soared
      popping their pyrotechnic
            buttons
The breathing of the tides
      the salty, sandy air
            the night wind
I took for granted
      puzzled-
            where was sensation?

We talked, clutched
        we petted
              all in ritual.
Now I stalked the border
        of the Hudson River park
              thousands butt to butt
Jammed on beaches
        watching the Jersey sky
              for fiery July 4 tremors.
I shook a thousand hands
        seeking treasured names
              for my Mayoral petition
Following in the wake
        of other candidates
              voters sitting ducks
And remembered
        the night
              and remembered the girl
Her lips and mine
        dry as the shore
              yet to feel the tides.

Old People Vote

The old lady, wheel-chaired,
her mottled grey face distorted
besides her, an old man, fidgetting,
his cane shifting hand to hand
two of dozens assembled in this limbo of last years
to hear politicians discourse.

(For them, what an event campaigning must be
and what tales to tell their children!)

Remember my grandfather, my grandmother
creases, wrinkles, liver marks, badges of love--
I could relate, sing to them
with the eloquence of understanding. Even love.
So I did. Their belief, their trust
radiated back. I felt warmth.
That old lady -- who stared at me so raptly --
could have been my blood.
If my hands could heal...

When I was done, questions, please --

The old lady, haltingly, asked:
"Are you the doctor?"

"Bernstein, you vote
for Bernstein,"
the chubby, raven-eyed
brunette who ran the Home
warned the old man going to the polls.
"Bernstein," she said again.

Later, when he returned,
she asked --
   "Did you vote?"
   He nodded.
   "Who for?"
   A pause. A blink, An answer --
   "Goldstein."
   "But I said Bernstein!"
   "Goldstein Bernstein,
   what's the difference?"
And he hunched his way to the parlor and its steeping tea.

Campaign Pitch

Come with me and my
   lover be
and I will ply you with
   secrets
of how garbage is collected
   and potholes patched.
Access, if you wish, the deepest
   fiscal recesses
bonds, assessments, boards
   of every kind --
Mata Hari be. And if elected,
   like a torrent
will I disgorge such knowledge
   you care to trade
asking now only for this night
   and the soft warm home of you.

A Politician's Prayer

I summon the ghosts of Jews
Italians, Greeks, Germans past.
I exhort the ancestors of the Lebanese,
Chinese, Nipponese and Ceylonese.
I cajole all those who haunt
the Turks, Brits, Laps, Swedes,
Spanish, Danish, Cornish and many others.
Oh! mighty congregation
of strains and brains that fiber our society
who we exalt above all other
setting no idols before thee,
we beseech your blessing, your loving care,
your kind consideration of everlasting life
and the votes of those whose living flesh
you now inhabit.
                    Amen.

Bed-Stuy

I said to the political club in Bed-Stuy
"Your children need the best teachers."
They said, "We need the jobs."
I said: "Your children must be able
            to compete".
They said:
"We need to eat today."
Later I saw the inside of the back room.
The leader was sizing me up.
For what?
He was friendly but not persuaded.
Not even enough to request a contribution.

Street Money

There is the campaign
and the street campaign.
The people
and the street people.
The money
and the street money.
The money has its ways.
Present
and unaccounted for.
It trickles into blocks
and bends around corners.
It is a poster, a permit, an errand.
It is a reason, a fact, a kindness.
Though powerful, it cannot save.
There is the word.
It slips around alleys,
sits on stoops,
passes through locked doors.
This is the word of the people,
judgment come to call.

Bensonhurst

The judge, almost frail, a deacon
of a man, cried vengeance
to the Bensonhurst crowd, milling
in the summer night, the festival light
and laughter a block away.
He campaigned for borough office
speaking only Italian, fanning
ashes of envy into flames.
I understood little of what he said
but I heard the rumble,
the muffled roar of some vast energy,
strong, ominous, rising in crescendo.
Then there was movement, like a herd pawing,
shouldering, edging to break free.
Then the Mayor spoke --
Zuccotti, Ameruso, Scoppetta --
his litany of the appointed
his testament to the blood of the people.
But the names were spikes in their hearts.
No tokens now!
A light wind whipped their faces,
a torrent raged in their breast.
Mario Cuomo commanded the platform:
"You are the sons of giants...
"Your fathers built this city...
"You are the royalty of honest work..."

He restored the peace of dignity.
I should have spoken next.
The microphone was not offered.
Instead, the crowd was dismissed
to filter back into the Brooklyn night.
I was a candidate to the wind and the stars,
speechless witness to a rite
no less ancient for its being now
purging demons from the tribal soul.

Later when I strolled the festival
people plied me with pasta and pastry.
Here was gaiety, wheels of fortune,
ladies with dazzling eyes and summer
white dresses, gallant young men beside them.

Many knew my name, wished me well.
This world, so far, a block away.

I Heard a Psalm

Sung in a Bed-Stuy church.
She said, this old black lady,
"I can't stand any of them.
They steal, they pander, everyone
knows it. But no one will
vote against them, those politicans.
They get votes because they are black.
Mine, too, I suppose.
But my daughter won't be caught.
she's going to be a nurse. She's training now."

I walked with Herman Badillo towards the park
where the platform was set up to hear the speeches.
There wasn't much of a crowd.
Some black kids eyed us curiously,
One, bold enough to approach me --
"Are you Percy Sutton ?" he asked.
Ah Percy, I thought, your cause is lost.

It was described as middle income housing
              in Queens.
So I was surprised to see a black audience
              sad, silent.
A small shopkeeper had just
              been killed.
Shot by a black teenager, a hoodlum.
Before me, leaders of the tenant patrol
of the school advisory board, the board of directors --
Could I give them a message of hope?
When I was not expecting an audience like this
              at all?
They said to me -- why can't we defeat
              ourselves?

Why are we trapped? Unable to move up?
I fumbled for lines --
but I knew they would be as hollow as the old
                    barrel at Coney Island's steeplechase
which, turning over and over, defied you
                    to walk without falling.
They said: We work hard. We send our kids to
                    school. We get small shops.
                    Small jobs. We go no further.
                    What must we do?
Glibness is all. Others would have an answer.
Speak to the issue.
            Tell it like it is.
                    Like it should be.
Say something.
I had tears. I had no answers.
Therefore, no words.
I am no politician.

After the black-out when the great night descended
the animals prowled the streets smashing and
                    snarling,
their ferocity unleashed against the oppressor,
                    civilization.

On the Satmar side, orderliness, nothing disturbed.
On the other side, chaos, rubble, wreckage.

The elder rabbi said to me: with baseball bats, we
walked the perimeters.
"No one passed..."
"Did they try?"
"No one passed."

They were proud of their new Mikva, an achievement.

continued

His office, over a meat market, teeming with
                    families, children.

A young, bearded reb talked knowingly of politics
                    -- he was a political agent.

They did not sense power in me. They wanted protection
                    against crime.

Would I start a movement? But no votes.

Death was a player in this election.
He/she took the role of bomb-thrower,
                    terrorist
Son-of-Sam, random killer, women
                    his target,
pop-eyed headlines his Boswell.
In Brighton Beach, where Sam stalked
                    I targeted
the sunswept, lotion-layered audience of
real voters -- almost all lever pullers,
voting their ethnic pastime.
My voice floated out over the huge pool,
                    the sun decks
the coming and going of the swimmer
                    and soda sipper;
the old Jews who had seen it all,
                    the young Italians
revelling in the newly-found good life,
                    up from beach and boardwalk.
Limp, gleaming tan, legs twitching,
                    a hum of conversation
a dry wind off the shore, crying gulls, a rasping
                    sound system --

is it possible to reach the human
                    heart
in this fortress of self-content?

And when I was done, some said
                    good luck; some looked, so what?
Who are you? Why are you? You dare to
                    challenge the union
who has given me
                    this chair in the sun?

Where do you find a crowd in the summer
                    heat?
The pools of Riverside? The baseball
                    park? Or Central Park?
The subways, rattling under, over ground --
Do these people vote?

Death always found its crowd, and its
                    politician
who says it speaks for me, that I am its
                    master.
Death drove the people of Brooklyn
                    their backs to the sea
in cottages and sun-salted
                    apartments
to deny their heritage. Drove
                    evil forces to prey on them.
Death is in the night, slick
                    as Son of Sam's bullet
or the gleaming shards of exploded windows,
                    bombs in the bank,
or the shattered lights or walls of the
                    night when darkness ruled,

continued

power failed. With it reason. The animals
                    preyed, their keepers in
      the cages.
Who has rhetoric for this? Who speaks
                    for strength?
Who says I will rule, tame, subject
                    to the lash, drive off the
                    barbarian.
Who says this unmistakably, yet surgically, wins.
Here where once great, beefy
                    resonant
socialists cried out for human
                    rights
I heard the chant of death
                    stop them.
Cry, cry for capital punishment.

No television came to cover me
or to ask a concession speech
Afterward, one of our few, committed suicide.
He, the loner, found no peace
in our lonely crusade.
Others found jobs; they who were lovers
made their way, if such there is.

Two winners in a run-off wanted more,
my smile as medals for their campaign.
An independent endorsement they felt.
What did I prove? My own destiny
                    no doubt.
Do not seek grace in politics.
Only the grim, hard necessity
                    of the politician.

The Uncommitted

There are those
sitting on boardwalk benches
who refuse to shake
my politician's hand.
 They turn away.
 They ignore me.
I do not speak their language.
 Russian
 Spanish
 Greek
 Italian
Or, perhaps, they understand too well.
(I, who am not a politician
am now a politician.)
Perhaps they are wise
to nurse their strength against the day
they must smash
 the teeth that shred
 their dignity.
Though they sit on the same benches
as those who eagerly reach out
to shake hands, exchange a word
who accept the system
and its lesions for its comfort-
there is something in their sullenness
more powerful than a religious vision.
I think
 our future preens for them
 alone.

If You Are a Candidate

I solemnly sputtered Armenian words
into a sea of candles lit for martyrs.
I clasped the hands of people
who sought a blessing
or relief from their housing problem.
I came to bandstands and parks
where relaxing people were eager to talk.
I climbed Coney Island's boardwalk ramp
where the Habana-Gila sifted through
                    the ocean air
and the raucous Russian sound of argument.
I called out at ballparks and barbecues:
Vote for me. Vote for me.
I gave my word.

A politican has no more to give,
so soon forgotten.

There are restaurants of ritual,
squares and plazas
festivals and ceremonies.
There are a thousand symbols
of a vibrant people.

And there is you.

If you are a candidate
a special light falls on the
waters of the Narrows.
A special breeze stirs the trees
on neighborhood streets.
A great soundless song
plays its melody in your heart.
If you do not hear it, you should not have run.

Votes count.
But they are not all that count.

So many losers have won
and their poetry
is a tattered, rain-splashed
headline of deceit

New York Post,
August 13, 1977

TODAY
Showers 85
TONIGHT
Showers 70-75
TOMORROW
Showers 85-90
Details, page 2
TV: PAGE 27

NEW YORK POST

SATURDAY, AUGUST 13, 1977 25 CENTS   Vol 176. No. 227   © 1977 The New York Post Corporation

FINAL ★

Court curbs killer's hustling lawyer — Page 3

COUPLE SLAIN IN CAR ON L.I.

The New York Times,
August 9, 1977

Son of Sam imitator feared

New York City for more than a year
ice said they were also looking into the
that the killings might somehow be

A man's wallet and the woman's pocket-
ned large amounts of cash, the cops
ling to an unofficial source, they had
\$5000 between them.

identities were tentatively established
in the wallet and pocketbook, but police

But the drug scene was far from Suffolk Police Commissioner Donald Dilworth's mind as he
raced out of his house in Northport and sped to
Wyandanch to take personal supervision of the
investigation.

Later he met with Babylon Town Supervisor
Thomas Fallon at the First Precinct in Amityville.
"We had to determine whether this was another Son of Sam-type killer," Dilworth said. "Our
headquarters in Yaphank was besieged by hundreds
of calls from concerned citizens everywhere. They,
too, wanted to know what kind of a killing this was."

The gunman, spotted running from the scene
and carrying the shotgun, was believed to have
made his getaway in a cream-colored sedan.

The shots, Dilworth said, were fired from relatively close range.

Although the street was deserted when the
killer struck, he did not escape observation. At the
corner where the car was parked is the Bantam
Vinyl Industries plant, a sprawling modern factory
with a full night crew working inside.

It was believed that one or more of the em-
ployes heard the shots, saw the gunman flee and
reported what they saw to police.

The alarm issued for the wanted man described
him as being six feet tall, and black like his victims.

Dud Bomb Discovered in Midtown In Building Targeted by F.A.L.N.

By MARY BREASTED   *Aug 9 1977*

An unexploded bomb was discovered
yesterday in one of the buildings men-
tioned as a target last Wednesday by
telephone callers who said they were
speaking for the Puerto Rican terrorist
group known as the F.A.L.N. Two bombs
exploded that day, killing one man and
injuring seven other persons, and dozens
of bomb threats led to massive evacua-
tions of office workers.

The bomb discovered yesterday was at
the American Metal Climb
ing, 1270 Avenue of the
Street. It consisted of tw
mite rigged to a wat
stopped—and wires insi
velope. The police said
tell whether it had been
fore last Wednesday m
two other bombs explod

Inspector Robert J. H
Arson and Explosion Sq
unexploded bomb was fo
employee, who saw the d
a shelf outside an eight
and who, according to t
parently looked inside an
security."

In another developme
the 26-year-old Bronx

had been seeking for questioning about
the F.A.L.N. terrorist group, appeared
voluntarily at the Manhattan District Attorney's office yesterday afternoon. He
refused to answer any questions in an
interview with an assistant district attorney, and he was subsequently arrested
on weapons-possession charges.

The police said the discovery of the
newest bomb had prompted new searches

tery winners
Page 8

ay who they were until relatives made
tifications at the morgue in Hauppauge
in which they were killed in a \$19,000
es-Benz 300-D with beige leather up-
lice said the couple's attire also reflected

cumstances, one police source said, also
at "some kind of a meeting could have
gress, if indeed this had to do with

Sam's Plan: More Girls, More Blood

By WILLIAM FEDERICI

According to a rambling diary seized in his apartment,
accused mass murderer David Berkowitz intended to kill at
least a dozen more young girls and, had he not been captured,
contemplated planting an explosive in the World Trade Center
and mowing down fleeing occupants with a machine gun.

Berkowitz wrote of these plans in a series of 70 notes. He said
that the acts would be committed to satisfy "Sam's lust for young blood."

Berkowitz' writings have been pack-
ed to his defense lawyers and to a
prosecution-appointed psychiatrist.
They are expected to submit reports by
Oct. 6 on his competence to stand trial.

Informed sources said that Berkowitz' notes, written in long hand paper,
discussed in poetry form the reasons
for the alleged .44-caliber killer's attacks
on young women and how he had re-
ceived his commands from the mystery
dog Sam.

In one such note, Berkowitz alleged

ly wrote how he expected to shoot at
least four more victims in Queens, two
more in Brooklyn, two in Bergen County, N.J., two to Nassau County and one
on City Island in the Bronx.

At the end of this note, he allegedly
wrote that if these attacks did not satisfy "Sam's blood lust" then perhaps an
explosive should be set in the World
Trade Center where he would await the
results armed with a machine gun.

When he was captured last month,

Berkowitz allegedly told authorities
that if he failed to find a victim in
Riverdale he would head for Suffolk
County and indiscriminately shoot down
victims outside a discotheque with an
automatic weapon.

A semiautomatic rifle was seized by
police along with the .44-caliber Bulldog
revolver allegedly used to kill six persons and wound seven over a 13-month
period.

While psychiatrists from Kings
County Hospital already have submitted
reports stating that the 24-year-old
former postal clerk is not competent to
stand trial, the court has granted the
Brooklyn district attorney's office per-
mission to allow another psychiatrist to
examine all of the evidence and examine the suspect.

Meanwhile, Brooklyn Supreme Court
Justice Leonard Yoswein said that he
would hold hearings this week to deter-

Holiday Toll Less Than '76

The Labor Day holiday death toll
on the nation's highways was 489,
well under last year's figure, a final
count showed yesterday.

The toll this year also was one
less than the National Safety Coun-
cil's prebeliday estimate of at least
470 persons — and possibly as many
as 570 — dying in traffic accidents.

A UPI tabulation showed that in
addition to the traffic deaths, 44 persons drowned and 12 were killed in
plane crashes — a total of 525 acci-
dental deaths between 6 p.m. local
time Friday and midnight Monday.

mine whether tapes of conversations between Berkowitz and his former lawyer
can be sold to the highest bidder.

---

pard of Ed

its plan for a change in
schools by December,
the mayoral election. If
the election, his succes
or reject the recomme
commission, but time is
because the current ter
Education expires in Ju

The Board of Educa
other lay board in the

Democratic mayoral candidates (from left) Bella Abzug, Herman Badillo, Mayor Beame, Mario Cuomo, Joel Harnett, Ed Koch and Percy Sutton
debate the issues at the St. Moritz Hotel last night.

Daily News, September 7, 1977

9
Lament

Riis

Jacob Riis
who has a park
named for him

in Brooklyn
was a journalist
at the turn

of the century
(nineteenth)
who patiently

made pictures
of New York
poverty.

He wasn't
after art
yet he created

a documentary
style
photographers

still remember
and his images
of the poor

on the streets
in their hovels
and sweat shops

aroused
a city to
their despair.

Today
in front of
Grand Central

or across
from the U.N.
or Ninth Ave

or whatever
warmth
blows up

thru gratings
pictures still
abound

waiting
for their album
their Riis.

Potamkin

At the base of the hill
        a man in a car beckoned,
                where is Potamkin?

I pointed to the showroom
        of the Cadillace dealer
                overflowing with people.

A Cadillac was draped
        with the American flag.
                Earnest sales persons.

Leaned foward in oral combat
        palaver stroking the air
                of national recession.

Was this a special promotion?
        Had I missed some radio
                or TV commercial?

Where was the hype lady
        with the blonde hair
                who solds the goods?

Walking around the corner
        into a cantankerous rain
                spewing puddles, dismembering umbrellas.

I sidestepped a sack
     Z-shaped, a humanoid
          its head in a cellar window

Wrapped in translucent sheets
     a small creature, grubbing warmth
          his soaking-wet boots curling,

Sleeping through unemployment
     soaring deficits, cutbacks
          and the stumbling rain.

Then to my garage where for
     $200 a month I could,
          should I desire,

Shield the bounty
     of Potamkin's most
          generous discount.

Potamkin In Ruins

Smoke curled from skyscrapers
steaming funnels of glass, steel, concrete.
Huge cavities gapped
the great jaw of the city.
Herpes seared its face.
And in the streets the homeless in rags
gagged in the shadows
rotting bodies mirroring their desolation.

Potamkin in ruins pondered it all.

It was the free ion movement,
the radicals, he blamed.
Life or death, they shrieked.
Choose one. Choose the other. It is
                              the same.
He had heard the murmur, heard
                              the tirades.

From some single, solemn gesture
a tattered shroud flicked
over the city, rain threatened.
A rack of thunder, jets of lightning.
A chalky film speckled the streets.
A confetti of ash silted the gloom.

Man the molecules, man the molecules
screamed personal computers
who saw their linkages in jeopardy,
their genetic bases under siege.

Potamkin in ruins recalled it all.

Once a star gleamed golden in the night
to be obliterated by scrofulous clouds
seeded with chaos and the charisma
                              of politicians.
Infrastructures with their endless pipes
                              and tracks
cracked open to tremulous roars.
Clones, their templates of DNA shredded,
                              like rag dolls
foundered on the crevasses and spiney
                              fissures
of the deranged. Where was hope?

Potamkin in ruins did not know.
Had long since stopped caring.
Then the rain, the destroyer, pounding
                              bullets
of rancid, obscene images.
Then there was a pause, then
                              a mild breeze
But there was almost no one to feel it.

Except, of course, Potamkin.

I Believe

Bullets spoke to me
when they said hello to JFK.
The editor cried.
The technician could not believe
       would not believe.

TV spoke to me
when Ruby's shadow pulled a
gun/exit Oswald.
The world would not believe
       seeing is believing

Moscone, Ryan, King
Wallace knew the bullets too.
They are museums.
Bobby Kennedy lectures there
       it's not hard to believe.

A South Bronx drug king
was sawed in half
on the very same altar
of the very day we fell in love.
               I said I believe.

Lament

The state's most
powerful leader
a convicted felon

changed the rules
to keep
his political job

a child molester
congressman
abuses corporate funds

a senator
a mayor
a councilman

a congressman
all are convicted
of taking bribes.

Is this not
the generation
to whom the torch

was passed?
What is there
about politics

or poetry
I am not
remembering?

10

Coney Island Mirrors

Coney Island Mirrors

There are those
        who remember
                the movies started here.
And the Astoria studios
        a memory of nickelodeons
                and penny arcades
When Brooklyn
        was home of the stars
                and Queens their studio.
Now Astoria lives again.

(Is not memory
        a movie
                self-created?)

And now television
        and now cable vision
                and now home video
With its big screen images
        looming,, zooming
        lingering
shadows of the Gods.
(And the TV networks are here.)

continued

So the image is bigger now
        than we are
                infinite now
And in its shifting base
        we pile uncertainties
                we call reality
or memory.
We are fragment-tortured
        minds of jig-saw pieces
        patternless
Our memory a
        deceiving maelstrom
                with a shiny surface
shimmering;
A movie whose
        serial images are in -
                out of sync.
Like Ragtime, Doctorow's
        imagining
                of people, times, events
Signalling a memory
        that was, wasn't
        could, might have, didn't
happen.
Isn't the movie
        a memory
                now visible?

Ourselves, distorted,
        in Coney Island mirrors
                endless fascinations
with ourselves
        or fragments of ourselves?

See now revolution
        (in whose memory?)
                in flashing imagery.
Is it really
        an exaltation of love -
                as in Beatty's Reds -
Aliens finding glory
        in the madness
                in each other?
Or is it Dr. Zhivago's
        love destroyed
                but not of country
his sorrow a national monument?

Which of us
        will make which image
                history?